and all of us drinking the blood of our enemies

poems

I0518648

john sweet

And All of Us Drinking the Blood of Our Enemies
Copyright © John Sweet 2025
ISBN: 979-8-9925009-5-0
Library of Congress Control Number: 2025938390

Editor: Michele McDannold

Roadside Press
Colchester, Illinois

Table of Contents

i. *this is not my century, but it's the one i will die in*

ii. always nailed to the cross of someone else's failures

iii. *somewhere between an uncertain truth and a tempting lie*

And everyone looks like a tombstone to me
—Tess Parks

i.   this is not my century, but it's the one i will die in

preface

and you can't be honest unless you're
writing poems no one will
ever read,
and even then you're a liar

even then
you've still missed the point

running dry

and then uncertain sunlight gives way to
grey skies in
the land of missing fathers

rooftops and treetops and then the cemeteries
at the edges of these slowly
fading upstate towns

the fact that god is neither a
question nor an answer

woman is stabbed to death by her lover

child is left behind in the burning trailer

no mercy shows the way to no future
but yet here we are

thief of light
becomes the king of crows

steals the blood from corpses to paint his
slogans on prison walls and

what are your choices?

will free will carry you past the palace gates
and out into the kingdom?

don't scream if you
don't want to be heard

don't pray when action is needed

all it ever sounds like
is surrender

and all of us drinking the blood of our enemies

class violence/awake

or this fucker who tells you
you'll need to suffer
if you ever want a brighter future

how easily
his bones can be broken
in the here and now

[and friendly faces with put-on smiles]

all the junkies
blinking in the sunlight
telling you it's time to get clean

asking if you have
any money

just something to get them
through til
the end of the week

because your government is your enemy; a poem for young children

all your fucked up sweethearts laughing in
the year of the plague because
no one's gonna make it home alive

because nothing matters when
everyone suffers

it's 3rd grade math, okay?

kid pulls the trigger and
his little sister is dead

good times on the dance floor, or maybe
stoned and naked in the weeds out
behind the blood factory

someone's idea of romance

someone's daughter on her hands and knees
while the camera zooms in on her ass

land of the free, right?

home of the brave

wealth of power because
anything less is failure

because anyone who tells you otherwise
                              hates america

and fear is a weapon, of course,
and pain is a tool,
and all your latest lover really wants is
a piece of your suicide

maybe the book but probably
the movie,
because the written word is a fool's game

maybe the soundtrack, but the songs
all gotta have that steady beat,
a catchy chorus,

get even the raped and the starving
tapping their toes

get even the dealers and
the junkies singing along

bring us all together,
one nation under god

the minotaur in defeat

simple and holy in the first
bright light of day,
the wolves asleep the children
devoured and will you put on
your blood-red dress?

will you comb the feathers
from my hair?

listen

we'll fall and we'll fuck and
we'll split the difference
between trust & love

we'll bury the past and
we'll burn the future

maybe build something more
hopeful from the soft grey
ashes of our hearts

[everyone was gay]

let sex be god and let sex be
the devil, or maybe just
let it depend on who you fuck

ask frankie b about this

ask j christ

the good times are always coming,
but they never seem to arrive

cobain dies
and then my father
and i can still remember where i was
when i heard the news both times

i can still remember that it was
all brought to me by strangers

that the girl in bed raised her
head, asked where the hell i was going,
but my answer escapes me

and this was the year in the trailer out
between the freeway and the river

always the sounds of trains in
the distance
like some de chirico painting

always a reason for a few more
lines of crank,
and it was no real surprise when
chrissy's boyfriend finally went off
the deep end and shot her

it was no one's fault that the baby
drowned in the tub, in the
sense that it was everyone's fault

and tony kept calling from the motel
on the other side of town to say
his wife had kicked him out,
to hint that he was looking for
somewhere else to stay, and i knew that
i'd been here too long

and all of us drinking the blood of our enemies

i knew that i'd have to
go visit my mother

that she'd tell me what a
fucking waste my life was

and i was already thinking ahead to
thirty years in the future

i was already planning to
prove her right just to become
the perfect version of my
father's only son

[am i untruthful?]

or you die alone surrounded by
everyone you ever loved or
you just die alone

we all do at least once,
and you make it look easy or
you screw it up every
step of the way

with any luck, you move past
the casual violence of childhood

tommy pritchard on his scraped &
bleeding knees, crying, being
told he's gonna suck that
cock *or else*

matt on the floor of the bus,
eyes rolled to the back of his head
because it wasn't a tic tac someone
left on the seat for him to find

and a house on fire is a
house on fire, right?

drunk man's gotta sleep just like
anyone else, and no one
could ever remember the baby's name

1975, i'm thinking,
and me with my black eye

babysitter with her haze of
cigarette smoke and her smell of pot,
laughs, tells me it's okay to put my
head between her breasts

tells me it's okay to kiss them,
and who am i gonna tell about this
without the shit hitting the fan?

no one, that's right, and so
fear gives birth to silence but
at least the days continues to pass

at least the idea of escape finds
room to take on weight and form

i learn to
grow my wings in secret

the minotaur, enlightened

down these dim sunlit hallways holding
the hands of sullen ghosts

no love = no addictions

do you see the appeal of
sleeping with liars?

of cages built from
stained glass bars?

no one's afraid to bleed if death is
just another form of dreaming
but i can't live like that

i need the forest and
        the forest's edge

i need the desert,
the abandoned factory,
the smooth expanse of lawn that leads
from sidewalk to picture window and
i need blue sky and soft white cloud

not a past that tastes like
a mouthful of blood

not a church filled with the
gnawed bones of innocent victims

are you with me here?

we are born flightless birds
but we evolve

understanding is a gift but my
generosity has reached its end

a man beyond the reach of despair is
a man finally safe at home

slow burn

or you and i and all the bluegrey
dreams of god that always seemed
to fade in the sunlight

the simple act of turning each of my
half-remembered summer afternoons into
something more profound than religion

not fear of growing old but
fear of days wasted

of the unknown being
worse than we'd ever imagined

you stand at the cliff's edge and jump
because this is how the story is written

addiction is an obvious answer

one hundred small deaths placed
end to end and said
the house is still empty

said *the truth is less beautiful than
all of the lies we tell when we're fucking*

says *the days will just keep growing
shorter until there's no time left at all*

a gift for the diamond eaters

in the desert and
still worried about drowning

in a room with crow
waiting for the news that some of my
fears might actually matter

waiting for a message from the
queen of open wounds but
it never comes

thirty years wasted in california and
then another thirty in upstate new york but
nothing you could call a life

blue skies and drunken phone calls

every letter ending
THIS WILL BE THE LAST LETTER and
all crow can do is laugh at the
stupidity of it

john sweet

drive up and down state line road
looking for the trailer park she
used to live in but
it's a different world these days

it's the ghost of morrison and the
ghost of cobain and the
memory of dancing to slow songs in
the half-light of the high school gym

the possibility of escape but
never the reality

endless days of sunlight
and never enough oxygen

never the sound of
anyone else's laughter

[submerged and unafraid]

the dream where this house is
slowly melting away like cardboard in a
heavy rain and then i wake up to
the fear of everything mixed
with impotent rage

the knowledge that my lies
will hurt others, but still i lie

still i manage to stand on my hind legs and
do a passable impersonation of a
wounded animal laughing like a human,
and good for me, right?

and less blood than usual
on the bathroom floor

three different types of pills to
keep me from imploding and
a fourth to keep the clocks all moving
                                    forward

small victories,
but i will claim them nonetheless,
and it was my first wife who
told me there were others

told me i didn't have to hate myself,
but i was pretty sure i did

and she told me she'd met someone else,
but i think i've mentioned this already

told me she was leaving

told me she was already gone

and the dates escape me, and nothing
ever happens in the order it
gets remembered

days pass and then they're forgotten,
and the kids just keep getting older

they go from innocent to sullen
to concerned,

and this is what terrifies me

they know something
or they suspect

they humor me when i remind them
i'm a poet,
when i show them my paintings

they disappear for weeks on end and i
forget their faces,
       their names,
         the reasons they had for leaving

i sit by a window in an empty room on
the 2nd floor and watch it rain

i feel the floor shift beneath me

hear water trickling down the walls and i
reach for my pills but find only a
yellowing pile of baby teeth

and i try to stand up
but my legs have no strength

my heart staggers drunkenly in my chest

misses a beat and then another
and i can't catch my breath

can't open my mouth to scream and
                        then i jerk awake

i wait for the day to
reassemble itself around me

for my heart to find its true rhythm

and i'm afraid

time, in the obvious sense

and it's your mother who finds
your father's body,
but it's a total stranger who
calls to break the news

it's your girlfriend in the hospital
and her sister in bed with you

it's the sister's best friend
asleep on the floor

and you think maybe she's the
one you actually love, but
the moment of hope
has already come & gone

late august, '93

or i tell him he's just a dying junkie in a
dying city and he laughs,
spits a mouthful of blood over the railing onto
the sidewalk three stories below, says
john you've always been the
biggest asshole i know

says *i've fucked every woman you've*
ever loved and none of it ever
meant anything

none of them ever gave a shit about
really being alive and then he
opens another beer

and then he
closes his eyes and smiles

[it's too late to be late again]

j christ and his
brother back in the summer of '74,
                              remember?

cemetery road where it dead-ends down by the
river and bowie on the tape deck, maybe
iggy, maybe t rex, and no one knows
the girl's name, of course

no one has any money for more
beer, and the pot's all gone

21ˢᵗ century just hangs there beyond the hills,
and not all of our father's end up
making it that far

not every story happens the way
we'll tell it to our kids

all that really matters in the end is that
there are always better ways to live

hymn

she says *let's pretend*
you're not my god
and he laughs

says *let's forget that the*
planes will crash or that
the baby will need a name and
she says these things and
the sky fills with rain

she believes in the future
even after it's
proven to be a lie

this is how he knows
he loves her

like a massacre of one

as many cans of spray paint as we
can steal, then huffing it out behind the
hardware store until tony starts puking, and so we
leave him there at the edge of the railroad tracks,
we walk away laughing, say *later faggot*, say
fucking pussy, and then we head down to
brockman's creek where jeannie and her
cousin like to hang out beneath
the route 9 bridge

says *where have you been, assholes?* and i smile,
say *lets see those tits* and she
gives me the finger

foreplay, right?

kingdom of nil in the first few months
of the new dark ages, and it's all just the fine art of
passing time until everyone is either passed out or
gone to
find something better, until the last few of us
remaining are
trying to convince the cousin to take off

her shorts, and i remember pulling the trigger
but i don't think i'm the one who
hits the dog

i remember it screaming, and the
sound of chris's laughter

says *you winged it!* says *we gotta kill it now* and he
wades after
it into the shallow water, tries to grab it while it
tries to bite him, and he looks over at me,
says *grab the gun, asshole,* says *grab a rock,*
and i just stare

i remember the future

remember totaling up all of my failures
on the day my oldest son is born

the weight of the sun and
the taste of blood
      of aspirin
      of orange soda spiked with acid
           but it's the past

        it's the here and now

the sound of cars passing overhead,
of chris trying to hold the dog underwater,
trying to drown it, laughing and shouting
get over here you fucking asshole! and
that dog is not going down

it just keeps on screaming

just keeps on bleeding

just keeps on diving headlong into
the age of blind forgiveness

bones, buried

fuck yr junkie deaths yr
crippled religions

no god here but
the god of crows

no windows in the room of
murdered children
because what would you see?

what song of false hope
would you expect to sing?

open yr mouth to offer a
prayer, but all that
ever comes out is
someone else's blood

my own worst enemy

dazed in the heat thinking it's
'74 again, thinking burroughs is still alive and
the garage is still on fire, and i have
remembered my entire life incorrectly but
there's the possibility it's
better this way

there are my sons and daughters who can
succeed where i've failed, and there is
a woman in california who once
mistook me for salvation

mixed me with pills and then lost
everything she had, and there is another
out there who sees me exactly as i am,
and what i do is fear them both

what i do is sit out in the back yard,
pinned down by the weight of the sun,
by the knowledge of my own
mortality, because listen

this is not my century,

but it's the one i will die in and
maybe you, too

we'll form a club

we'll get religion

immortality is attractive, sure, but so is
the idea of safety to anyone jumping
from the 98th floor of a burning building

gives you the illusion of comfort,
but it's just not gonna happen

and dead is dead, but we can still
find some laughs along the way

we can look for better
sex or bigger paychecks

we can crank t rex on the tape deck
and drive out to
the lake with a couple cases of beer

good times in the kingdom of nil

children locked in cages so the freedom
of the masses can be assured

all of the assholes in the world
who will tell you it
just can't be any other way

epilogue, early draft

and it takes me a long goddamn
time to figure out i'm too old for this shit,
that i'm past the point of caring,
february and freezing in the house where i'll be
found dead someday, and what i don't know
is if i'm saving up energy for one more
attack or if i've just started to fade away

what i don't know is what my father
thought of me at any point in my life,
                    and does it matter?

am i nothing more than the
sum total of my failures?

goddamn right
i am

*ii.   always nailed to the cross
of someone else's failures*

landscape with deeper truths

coyote skull easter sunday, says *this is*
not the moment says *the sun is all wrong is all*
snow on abandoned gas stations and i am
not the child i wanted to be and
we only ever became adults by necessity

the bills had to be paid
the bodies buried

mother said *yr father always*
loved you
but she looked at the floor

1985 or 86 and the creek
sweeps away the beggar's house

two burnout assholes i go to school with
are trapped on a steadily disappearing island
in the middle of the river

days into months into years until
i grow tired of my name
        of my face

but the future can't be stopped

monday morning thick with fog but then
a pale yellow brilliance by noon
a drive home through
hesitatnt early-evening rain

splintered wood and rusted metal where
the trailers used to be
and always the sound of crows

always the possibility of bliss

the need to choose between
FUCKED and FUCKED UP

can't waste every sunlit morning worrying
that yr heart is a desert but
what if it is?

just the bones of christ and the
song of judas, just endless expanses of
late winter blue sky beauty

flags without meaning, just color and shape

just vultures circling

the animal brought down
by the first shot

suffering but not yet dead

man with his rifle and his
meaningless smile
contemplating the simple joy of life

poem on the eve of

and we all want to be
god but none of us
wants to be christ, and each
day colder than the
      one before it

each one brighter, and
we have almost reached the
shore but we are lost

we have eaten the children,
and now we are starving

now we are dying such
ordinary deaths

on the road to the sun

no apologies for the
dream of severed hands

let the rooms fill with water and
the walls melt like cardboard

let the fields be buried
beneath piles of rotting corpses

tell your children this isn't the
future you wanted for them but
what did you ever do to stop it?

how many people do you have
to kill to stop the killing?

wait your whole frightened life
for the punchline but
it never comes

and all of us drinking the blood of our enemies

other shades of nil

unborn child takes a bullet
between the eyes but
i'm still working on the punchline

i'm still trying to explain the
humor in the
news of the drowning boy

i'm still in love with every
wasted day you and i
ever spent together

it's a life, yes,
but it's no way to live

the blind eye

the approximate wilderness of
me to you, of shadows cast on sunwashed
five below zero january afternoons

said *can't waste your whole*
life in empty rooms with
a gun to your head

says *can't put your*
faith in the dirt-smeared
wisdom of junkies

a mouthful of road salt at
3 in the afternoon

dull scrape of
frozen metal on frozen metal and that
there's nothing we can do but laugh at
whoever puts their future in the
hands of the wrong idiot god

fucked

and all of us drinking the blood of our enemies

is fucked

dig at the heart of your latest lover
with rust-stained fingers

talk about trust while the blood
pours from your favorite wounds and
                                    listen

do you remember mia's body
found in its christ pose
outside the comet?

do you remember how we knew that
the days of wonder had
come to an end?

year zero in the age of naught

my father kept telling me
i needed to grow up
kept stopping by my two-room apartment
drunk and confused
in the middle of the afternoon

wanted to sleep on my couch

said he'd need a place to stay if
things didn't get better with my mother

said he knew that my sister was the
root of all his problems and
the kid behind the counter didn't
deserve to die but the
same can be said for a lot of us

the past is nothing but ruins,
the future just a
fist through a plate glass window

the woman i love says she
will forgive me anything and i
was talking about faith here

i was justifying my own hatreds
                              but not yours

no kingdom has ever been
built on a foundation of mercy

let the idea be the map, let the palaces all burn

born beneath stubborn hills,
near barren water

no faith but the
faith we create, right?

cities as mausoleums

poetry written in semen

find just one person in your
life with the gift of vision but
never learn her name,
                    or worse

learn her name, but only
when it's too late to matter

middle-aged and lost in the
desert of upstate new york and
where the hell have you ever been but
this particular slice of nowhere?

how much of your life have you
wasted believing that
falling in love would
be the act that saves you?

look

the days have always been
beyond our control

the wolves keep circling
closer around the children, but
they wait for a signal

whichever man tells you
no one needs to die
is the one to kill first

how many other rules
could we possibly need?

nought from aught

a straight line between the past i regret
and the future you fear

and we talk about love,
and we speak from our hearts,
and then we go home to our families,
and this is how the summer passes

distance made tangible

despair disguised as wisdom

a nation built from splinters of the
one true cross, and it can
only collapse on itself in the end

laughing matter

or if i was a poet offering
easy answers
or if i was a god

if we met for the first time
four years before my father died

created love out of nothing
and then threw it away

figured we could find it again
if we needed to

didn't realize we were wrong
until after
the baby was born

and every day a day for assassination

suicides and lovers and
the point where they overlap

blue skies and good times
in the plague years

poison, sure, but not enough for everyone,
and so how do you decide?

how big a forest can be grown
with just one small cupful of blood?

let's not bullshit each other here

everyone believes in violence

everyone knows the beatles
couldn't hold a candle to the stones

they know democracy is a lie

vote one way or the other,

but you're always fucked straight up
the middle in the end

you're always nailed to the
cross of someone else's failures

brings a smile to your face when
you finally realize that it hurts
even worse than you thought it would

the oblique

sunlight in the
spaces between houses

map of loss

geography of both
memory and sorrow and
then what?

find the man with the
crosses carved into his palms

find the one with the head of
a crow,
with the mind of a jackal

the junkie hymns are
what matter here,
and the prayers
of murdered dreamers

gold and myrrh and that
all gifts are weapons

that all lovers
believe in resurrection

the heart betrays the body
                    yes
but then the
body betrays the soul

ecstasy precedes despair

the desert spreads without
mercy in every direction

and all of us high in the age of heretics

learn the language of failure

learn the subtler methods of violence

12 years old kid with a gun
shoots his father dead

band breaks up but
the records keep selling

money for lawyers and
money for dope,
and no one finds the singer's body
until two weeks after his OD

nothing burns so brightly as
the witch you fear the most

[beyond the glare, there's burning everywhere]

or else step off the
ledge to see if you can fly

breathe and then pause and
are we in love here?

were we ever?

look

once you let truth get in
the way of reality,
you're fucked

once you let the dogs get a
taste for human blood,
the future is torn wide open

learn to crawl

learn to hide

there is no safer place to

be than the trigger-end of a gun,
and was it cobain who
told us this?

how can you *not* laugh?

how could the sun
ever refuse to shine on all of
the cowards of this world?

we are all so
desperately beautiful in
that last endless second
before the sky begins
                    to fall

eventually, new empires

it was always the wrong time, you
were always the wrong lover

it was the sound of laughter,
of footsteps in the hallway

it was winter

a child asleep in a house on fire, and
are you tired of that story yet?

listen

nothing new ever rises
from the ashes

no one steps into the light at
your lowest moment to
tell you you matter

it might be time to stop
waiting for a sign and just get
on with your life

[tell him that the truth will help him live with less]

says the past is depressing, says
thinking about the future just
makes him suicidal,
does another line of crank,
and this is friday night
at tony b's

gotta play all the angles just right
if you want to fuck his girlfriend

got to explain to his sister
how it didn't mean anything

gotta hope he doesn't
come looking for blood when
the whole goddamn house
of cards falls down

[shallow and blind]

everyone says they're
sorry you're dead,
but everyone lies

they dream of
fucking you up the ass

they believe the
drugs will work, but
listen –

it's not gonna be the
summer of '94
forever

phone's gonna ring,
but it won't be kelly

it won't be trish

at some point,
everyone grows up,

gets a life,
leaves this town

at some point,
everyone
loses the point

they get the news
of your death

they weight what it
might mean for them
in the possible
future

it matters that not
everyone
gets to
end up a winner

....and shovels held high

in the world of
overdosed junkies
the living man is king

get it?

and just because you're
crying doesn't mean
it's not funny

song of hope

and the billionaires aren't going to save you
because giving a shit about anyone else
isn't how you become a billionaire,
but watching those fuckers die,

                    now

that's a whole other
level of salvation

fanfare for starving dogs

dead king on a burning throne

do you remember this
freakshow?

gotta choose between
getting high or being depressed, and
i will always be the opposite
of my father

man couldn't drink that
gasoline fast enough

hands too shaky
to light the match

no worse time to be alive
than the age of human kindness
but how would any
of us know?

babies choking on shards of glass

pretty girls with their
sympathetic smiles and a
desert outside every door but
at least he had the bottle

my father, you understand

not quite a blind man and
not quite a prophet

a believer in the
mathematics of straight lines

in directions chosen

drive 100,000 miles in
whatever direction feels right and
what choice do you have but
to end up anywhere else?

poem as self-evident truth

and death does not = great art
but don't tell the dead man this

let the fucker bleed a little more

let the neighbors wake up
                too late
        in a house on fire

there is no loss so great it could
ever compare to your own

everything is wrong and it's all someone else's fault

a pale white sun in a silver sky and
all of the emptiness where
everything that hides
hides in plain sight

all of your father's despair and
all of his self-pity,
which is what he left you when he died

had a smile on his face when you
found the body, but that
might've just been the drugs

might've just been the simple joy
of floating up above the pain

*iii.   somewhere between
an uncertain truth and a
tempting lie*

[just a rock'n'roll joe with tales of woe]

in the slow truth of broken afternoons,
waiting for warmth, waiting
for sunlight or at least for the names of my
children to be returned to me, and
are you a believer?

have you learned to embrace the
politics of ignorance?

picture this

a sunday afternoon somewhere in
the first few weeks of autumn

a dying factory town, further upstate

and no one here speaks of
de chirico,
but his ghost is everywhere

no one speaks of cobain, but they've
all bought his t-shirts at walmart

they turn 30, then 40, then 50

they stand down by the river waiting for
the bones of indians, of missing
children, of old lovers to wash ashore,
and do you understand why
all pain is funny?

look

it's okay to hate your government

it's okay to hate your parents

odds are, they were never that
crazy about you, either, and now you've
got this house you can't afford

you've got this job you can't stand

and you had friends at some point,
or at least drinking buddies,
but those days are gone

the past was wasted and the present

just slips through your fingers and
how could the future ever be anything
but more of the same?

powerlines and cell phone towers and
all of these potholed roads that
do nothing but turn back on themselves

you arrive here again
even as you leave

you are more or
less human

doesn't matter whose fault it is,
you will always be
the one who gets the blame

[i got mine, but i want more]

spend yr whole
fucking life
carrying this dead man
through some
neverending
desert

listening to these
asshole poets
whine about metaphors

about agents and
book sales, but
this dead man knows the truth

knows these days are
all that truly matter

knows
dead is dead

and all of us drinking the blood of our enemies

gonna lead you to
your grave knowing you
have no choice but
to follow him

here come the good times

and frankie b understands that
sometimes
you're a dead man

says *fuck love* or just
says *fuck* and
who are you to disagree?

not every act of hope is
guaranteed to survive

not every god
lives to see 28

and plan for success, sure,
but keep your options open

dig the hole deep enough to
bury everyone
you've ever loved

it's gonna come in
handy sooner or later

[all my friends are junkies; no, that's not really true]

there is nothing, or
there is nothing here

houses on fire, but invisibly

back yards green and freshly
mowed, but the bodies always
moving closer to the surface

young girls with brittle bones

poison sent down from
the castle

and no can believe the
truth if the
truth is kept hidden

do you see how that works?

no one can sing their
favorite songs once all of our
tongues have been cut out, and

do you remember all of those
times getting high with the
ghost of christ?

do you remember those
neverending summer afternoons
filled with sunlight and
ecstasy and blowjobs?

felt good knowing we were
going to live together, and then
we heard about cobain

then we heard about layne

watched those doomed
fuckers jumping from the 98th
floor, escaping one miserable death
only to be embraced by
another, and was mandy still
alive for this?

it seems like she was

seems like her suicide was still

and all of us drinking the blood of our enemies

in the early stages,
crying jags and tequila,
cheap-ass coke,
late-night phone calls to
whichever ex had fucked her
over the hardest,
but listen

there is nothing

there is nothing here

these are not the
same concepts

this is neither an
explanation nor an apology

we can only live without
hope
for a very short time

later, after the vivian girls have gone

summer of drugs,
same as any other

someone finds your lover dead,
then someone else becomes your next lover, and
this is both symmetry and poetry

not cherished, not
needed, but used

if it's all you've ever known
then it's all you'll ever recognize

a trailer out on burnt hill road

a dealer who understands the
necessary intersection
between sex and money

      give and take,
      give and take,
      give and
      take

philosophy, right? but on your
knees and with
your hands behind your back

some floyd on the stereo

another cranked-out asshole with a
gun and some rambling
interior monologue
walking up to the counter of the
mini-mart just as you open your mouth

and what is it that's ever
mattered more than
the truth?

in praise of hindsight

a slow, steady count back
down to zero and
how many lies did it take before we
came crawling back to the truth?

and it seems like we should
have had other choices

greed

the other lives that define your own
all stacked up around you

music, which = sound

joy, which is always in the past

and st maria looks over
your shoulder,
asks if the poem is for her,
                              but no

there's been a war here or,
at the very least,
a slaughter

the corpses of another 20 children
to help pave the road to peace

another girl named mandy found
dead on the highway somewhere

beteween here and the southern
border of the kingdom of nil

loved, maybe, or
maybe just fucked

just?

yes, it happens

emotion is never mandatory

ask the soldiers

ask the false king

let rape, let murder, let
all abuses of power be nothing
more than a means to an end

let hope be for the weak,
for the victims and
the temporary survivors

and all of us drinking the blood of our enemies

let whatever you want
be more than what
you have the right to ask for

crystal

a clean wind
through broken windows

shadows of clouds across the hills,
                    the freeways,
            the bright green back yards

saw you standing at
the desert's edge

heard the weight of truth
in your silence

said we are fucked but
so are our enemies and it wasn't
the drugs that made me smile it was
the sound of your heart

it was the wide open spaces between
the hilltops and the clouds

all of the secrets we
thought to hide there

the story i was told

leave your wife home
with the kid, right?

fuck it

these are the halcyon days

no past and no future and so
you drive to a different part of town and
you kick in her door

she laughs, tells you it's got to
stop at some point,
and you smile

you walk in and
start undressing her

there is no such
thing as time

just to see

and we could be christ,
sure, or we
could just be better

accept the fact that there is
limitless wealth to be found in
the deaths of others, and the
future becomes limitless

accept the failure of the past,
        the man-made corpses,
            the cities in flames,
but what do we have to offer
            for the future?

why do we just assume
there will be one?

understand yourself to
be a cancer, and
there are no more
mysteries left to solve

and all of us drinking the blood of our enemies

a psalm from his later years

always this doubt

always this nagging fear that
i've ended up becoming
my father despite
everything

when the drugs were still working in our favor

and all the pretty girls want to
die in the summer of '75,
and the kid across the street sets the
catholic church on fire

and what the fuck were we doing
wasting our lives in this
nothing corner of upstate new york?

grow up and grow old having done
nothing but bear witness to
our fathers' suicides

name our children after ourselves

teach them to hate us

give them maps

just enough money to help them
get as far away as possible

and all of us drinking the blood of our enemies

and every day is the best day at the death party

older kid down the street says you're
going to suck his cock or he's
going to start breaking your fingers

says the choice is yours, but smiles and
tells you he's starting to lose patience

[i dream as you can dream]

1973 and the
neighbor's house on fire

the babysitter stoned and
her boyfriend laughing

has his hand down her shorts,
tells you to turn the stereo up

tells you to get him
another beer out of the fridge,
and the sound of sirens
in the distance

the future not here yet,
but fucking unstoppable

just killing everything
in its path

[baby says she's going away]

we are dead men singing on
the morning of the funeral

we are christ after the
ascension is shown to be lie

are you with me here?

scrape of gunmetal against your
teeth is only one version of the future,
so sit back for a minute

what you own will always end up
being no different than
what you owe

everything i write will always
fall somewhere between an
uncertain truth and a tempting lie

and it's a trick, sure,
but everything is

your god has no substance, your
devil does only the things you
would if you weren't
afraid of getting caught

it's the best description of
religion you're ever going to get,
so live with it

look at the big picture

nothing we accomplish will
ever really make a difference

nothing we've created will
matter once it's all underwater, but
here we still are with our
canvasses, with our pens and paper,
our guns and bombs, our
collapsing walls, and at what point
does the future become a myth?

possibly before any of us
were ever born

maybe later

maybe the exact moment your
youngest child is shot to
death on a school playground

you build a house and
you call it home and then all
it does is burn

[we live through these times and never change the way we are]

and it's easy to understand why all
the politicians need to die,
but where do you go from there?

how much ecstasy does it take to
bring each day into focus?

how much blood to do you have to lose
before you start to become a better person?

and you know every last one of us
is fucked, but
all you do is sit there and laugh

and all of us drinking the blood of our enemies

[there you go again with all your useless conversation]

some fucking poet w/ his
head up his ass and
his girlfriend on her knees

wants to tell you his version of the
truth but all you want is to get high

all you want is to
sleep with his sister

convince her she's beautiful

make it to payday with
some gas left in the tank

endnotes

what you fail to learn from
history is how not to be poor

is how not to be powerless

what the future holds for you
isn't salvation but more
of the same

John Sweet, b. 1968, still numbered among the living. He's been running around unsupervised in the small press since around the time of Camper Van Beethoven's first break-up. Opposed to all organized religion and political ideologies, but he has a soft spot for existential nihilism. Mostly tries to avoid ending up on the side of the assholes and the bullies. It gets easier every year. The story of his life is buried somewhere in all of his writing.

MORE ROADSIDE PRESS TITLES

MORE ROADSIDE PRESS TITLES